Aviano Air Base
Beale Air Force Base
Davis-Monthan Air Force Base
Dyess Air Force Base
Eielson Air Force Base
Ellsworth Air Force Base
Fort Meade
Grand Forks Air Force Base
Hill Air Force Base
Hurlburt Air Force Base
Kadena Air Base
Kirtland Air Force Base
Royal Air Force Lakenheath
Little Rock Air Force Base
Luke Air Force Base
Malmstrom Air Force Base
Maxwell Air Force Base
Joint Base Lewis-McChord
Joint Base McGuire-Dix-Lakehurst
Minot Air Force Base
Moody Air Force Base
Osan Air Base
Peterson Air Force Base
Ramstein Air Base
Scott Air Force Base
Sheppard Air Force Base
Tyndall Air Force Base
United States Air Force Academy
Vandenberg Air Force Base
Wright-Patterson Air Force Base

Note: The appropriate disposition to sexual assault allegations and investigations may not always include referral to trial by court-martial. Rather, some cases may be more appropriately handled through adverse administrative accountability actions. Additionally, adjudged sentences reported herein do not reflect any relief on the sentence that may have been granted upon appeal.

Aviano Air Base

United States v A1C Corey L. Payton

Base: Aviano AB, Italy

Synopsis: After a night of drinking A1C Payton sexually assaulted the wife of a deployed coworker at her home after returning to the victim's home with several of their friends.

Trial Results: On 1 Oct 10, at Aviano AB, Italy, A1C Payton was convicted by general court-martial of rape using force.

Adjudged Sentence: A1C Payton was sentenced to confinement for 12 months, a bad conduct discharge, and reduction in rank to E-1.

United States v A1C Korey J. Talkington

Base: Aviano AB, Italy

Synopsis: After a night of drinking and watching movies, A1C Talkington sexually assaulted a female Airman while she was sleeping in his dorm room.

Trial Results: On 7 Oct 10, at Aviano AB, Italy, A1C Talkington was convicted by general court-martial of 3 counts of aggravated sexual assault.

Adjudged Sentence: A1C Talkington was sentenced to confinement for 8 months, a bad conduct discharge, reduction in rank to E-1, and total forfeiture of all pay and allowances.

Note: The appropriate disposition to sexual assault allegations and investigations may not always include referral to trial by court-martial. Rather, some cases may be more appropriately handled through adverse administrative accountability actions. Additionally, adjudged sentences reported herein do not reflect any relief on the sentence that may have been granted upon appeal.

Beale Air Force Base

United States v SSgt Todd J. Barlow

Base: Beale AFB, CA

Synopsis: SSgt Barlow committed various sexual offenses against subordinate female airmen.

Trial Results: On 24 Jun 11, SSgt Barlow was convicted by general court-martial of attempted aggravated sexual contact, attempted abusive sexual contact, forcible sodomy, indecent acts, indecent exposure, and 2 specifications of cruelty and maltreatment.

Adjudged Sentence: SSgt Barlow was sentenced to confinement for 3 years, a dishonorable discharge, and reduction in rank to E-1.

Davis-Monthan Air Force Base

United States v 2d Lt Charles L. Allen

Base: Davis-Monthan AFB, AZ

Synopsis: 2d Lt Allen was charged with sexual assault based on several allegations of aggressive behavior after meeting women through online dating services.

Trial Results: On 7 Mar 12, at Davis-Monthan AFB, 2d Lt Allen was convicted by general court-martial of aggravated sexual assault, making a false official statement, and conduct unbecoming an officer.

Adjudged Sentence: 2d Lt Allen was sentenced to confinement for 5 years, a dismissal, and a reprimand.

United States v SSgt Adrian G. Lara

Base: Davis-Monthan AFB, AZ

Synopsis: SSgt Lara and his victim, a female Airman, were previously in a relationship and have a son together. SSgt Lara visited the Airman at her duty location in Ohio to return their son to her after a vacation. That night, SSgt spent the night at the female Airman's home, she consented to sexual activity, but told SSgt Lara that she did not want to have intercourse. Despite her saying she did not want to have intercourse, SSgt Lara had intercourse with her.

Trial Results: On 28 Oct 10, SSgt Lara was convicted by general court-martial of 2 counts of rape and forcible sodomy.

Adjudged Sentence: SSgt Lara was sentenced to confinement for 5 years, a dishonorable discharge, and reduction in rank to E-1.

Note: The appropriate disposition to sexual assault allegations and investigations may not always include referral to trial by court-martial. Rather, some cases may be more appropriately handled through adverse administrative accountability actions. Additionally, adjudged sentences reported herein do not reflect any relief on the sentence that may have been granted upon appeal.

United States v SrA Joshua D. Hall

Base: Davis-Monthan AFB, AZ

Synopsis: While in Baltimore for one night returning from deployment to the AOR, a group of airmen went out drinking to celebrate their return home. During the night, SrA Hall and a female got separated from the rest of the group. While separated, SrA Hall punched the female Airman in the face repeatedly and raped her.

Trial Results: On 26 Feb 10, at Davis-Monthan AFB, AZ, SrA Hall was convicted by general court-martial of rape using force.

Adjudged Sentence: SrA Hall was sentenced to confinement for 8 years, a dishonorable discharge, reduction in rank to E-1, and total forfeiture of all pay and allowances.

Note: The appropriate disposition to sexual assault allegations and investigations may not always include referral to trial by court-martial. Rather, some cases may be more appropriately handled through adverse administrative accountability actions. Additionally, adjudged sentences reported herein do not reflect any relief on the sentence that may have been granted upon appeal.

Dyess Air Force Base

United States v SrA Danny M. Burns

Base: Dyess AFB, TX

Synopsis: After a night of drinking during a church retreat weekend, SrA Burns sexually assaulted a female airman in his apartment.

Trial Results: On 13 Nov 10, at MacDill AFB, FL, SrA Burns was convicted by general court-martial of forcible sodomy, and 2 counts of use of controlled substances.

Adjudged Sentence: SrA Burns was sentenced to confinement for 6 months, a bad conduct discharge, and reduction in rank to E-1.

Note: The appropriate disposition to sexual assault allegations and investigations may not always include referral to trial by court-martial. Rather, some cases may be more appropriately handled through adverse administrative accountability actions. Additionally, adjudged sentences reported herein do not reflect any relief on the sentence that may have been granted upon appeal.

Eielson Air Force Base

United States v TSgt Dennis D. Keller

Base: Eielson AFB, AK

Synopsis: After his wife spent an evening drinking with a female Airman, TSgt Keller and his wife brought the Airman to their home to take care of her due to her being substantially intoxicated. After TSgt Keller's wife went to sleep, TSgt Keller sexually assaulted the Airman while she was incapable of providing consent due to her level of intoxication.

Trial Results: On 28 May 10, TSgt Keller was convicted by general court-martial of 5 counts of aggravated sexual assault.

Adjudged Sentence: TSgt Keller was sentenced to confinement for 5 years, a dishonorable discharge, reduction in rank to E-1, and total forfeiture of all pay and allowances.

Note: The appropriate disposition to sexual assault allegations and investigations may not always include referral to trial by court-martial. Rather, some cases may be more appropriately handled through adverse administrative accountability actions. Additionally, adjudged sentences reported herein do not reflect any relief on the sentence that may have been granted upon appeal.

Ellsworth Air Force Base

United States v A1C Andrew C. Certa

Base: Ellsworth AFB, SD

Synopsis: A1C Certa sexually assaulted multiple women and interfered with the investigation against him.

Trial Results: On 22 Jul 12, at Ellsworth AFB, SD, A1C Certa was convicted by general court-martial of aggravated sexual assault, abusive sexual contact, forcible sodomy, obstruction of justice, false official statement, malingering, and dereliction of duty.

Adjudged Sentence: A1C Certa was sentenced to confinement for 3 years and 3 months, a bad conduct discharge, reduction in rank to E-1, and total forfeiture of all pay and allowances.

Note: The appropriate disposition to sexual assault allegations and investigations may not always include referral to trial by court-martial. Rather, some cases may be more appropriately handled through adverse administrative accountability actions. Additionally, adjudged sentences reported herein do not reflect any relief on the sentence that may have been granted upon appeal.

Fort Meade

United States v TSgt Danny L. Annis

Base: Ft. Meade, MD

Synopsis: TSgt Annis sexually assaulted the female spouse of an airman who spent the night at his house after a night of drinking.

Trial Results: On 22 Jul 11, at Ft. Meade, MD, TSgt Annis was convicted by a general court-martial of aggravated sexual assault, and abusive sexual contact.

Adjudged Sentence: TSgt Annis was sentenced to a bad conduct discharge.

Note: The appropriate disposition to sexual assault allegations and investigations may not always include referral to trial by court-martial. Rather, some cases may be more appropriately handled through adverse administrative accountability actions. Additionally, adjudged sentences reported herein do not reflect any relief on the sentence that may have been granted upon appeal.

Grand Forks Air Force Base

United States v AB Joshua Katso

Base: Grand Forks AFB, ND

Synopsis: AB Katso entered the dorm room of a female airman and sexually assaulted her while she was incapacitated from alcohol consumption.

Trial Results: On 6 May 11, at Grand Forks AFB, ND, AB Katso was convicted by general court-martial of aggravated sexual assault, burglary, and unlawful entry.

Adjudged Sentence: AB Katso was sentenced to confinement for 10 years, a dishonorable discharge, and total forfeitures of all pay and allowances.

United States v TSgt Alan K. Hohenstein

Base: Grand Forks AFB, ND

Synopsis: TSgt Hohenstein sexually assaulted the daughter of an airman who spent the night at his house.

Trial Results: On 26 Mar 11, at Grand Forks AFB, ND, TSgt Hohenstein was convicted by general court-martial of rape using force, and wrongful sexual contact.

Adjudged Sentence: TSgt Hohenstein was sentenced to confinement for 6 months, a bad conduct discharge, and reduction in rank to E-3.

Note: The appropriate disposition to sexual assault allegations and investigations may not always include referral to trial by court-martial. Rather, some cases may be more appropriately handled through adverse administrative accountability actions. Additionally, adjudged sentences reported herein do not reflect any relief on the sentence that may have been granted upon appeal.

Hill Air Force Base

United States v 1st Lt Brandon W. McClannahan

Base: Hill AFB, UT

Synopsis: After a night of drinking with 1st Lt McClannahan and his wife, 1st Lt McClannahan's subordinate, a female NCO, accused him of sexually assaulting her.

Trial Results: On 19 Aug 10, at Hill AFB, UT, at a general court-martial, 1st Lt McClannahan was acquitted of aggravated sexual assault, but convicted of indecent acts and fraternization.

Adjudged Sentence: 1st Lt McClannahan was sentenced to confinement for 30 days and a dismissal.

Note: The appropriate disposition to sexual assault allegations and investigations may not always include referral to trial by court-martial. Rather, some cases may be more appropriately handled through adverse administrative accountability actions. Additionally, adjudged sentences reported herein do not reflect any relief on the sentence that may have been granted upon appeal.

Hurlburt Air Force Base

United States v A1C Ricardo L. Pomales

Base: Hurlburt AFB, FL

Synopsis: In a hotel room rented by A1C Pomales, a female Airman and another male Airman, A1C Pomales exposed himself to the female Airman and sexually assaulted her after she and the other male Airman had consensual sexual intercourse in the hotel room.

Trial Results: On 5 Oct 10, at Hurlburt AFB, FL, A1C Pomales was convicted by general court-martial of indecent exposure and wrongful sexual contact.

Adjudged Sentence: A1C Pomales was sentenced to confinement for 12 months, a bad conduct discharge, reduction in rank to E-1, and total forfeiture of all pay and allowances.

Note: The appropriate disposition to sexual assault allegations and investigations may not always include referral to trial by court-martial. Rather, some cases may be more appropriately handled through adverse administrative accountability actions. Additionally, adjudged sentences reported herein do not reflect any relief on the sentence that may have been granted upon appeal.

Kadena Air Base

United States v A1C Nicholas R. Elespuru

Base: Kadena AB, Japan

Synopsis: A1C Elespuru sexually assaulted a female coworker who spent the night at his marital home after a night of drinking.

Trial Results: On 29 Mar 12, at Kadena AB, Japan, A1C Elespuru was convicted by general court-martial of abusive sexual contact, wrongful sexual contact, and assault consummated by battery.

Adjudged Sentence: A1C Elespuru was sentenced to confinement for 3 years, a dishonorable discharge, and reduction in rank to E-1.

Note: The appropriate disposition to sexual assault allegations and investigations may not always include referral to trial by court-martial. Rather, some cases may be more appropriately handled through adverse administrative accountability actions. Additionally, adjudged sentences reported herein do not reflect any relief on the sentence that may have been granted upon appeal.

Kirtland Air Force Base

United States v SSgt Christopher T. Chambers

Base: Kirtland AFB, NM

Synopsis: SSgt Chambers raped his ex-wife at knife-point in her home.

Trial Results: On 17 Jun 11, at Kirtland AFB, NM, SSgt Chambers was convicted by general court-martial of rape and assault with a dangerous weapon.

Adjudged Sentence: SSgt Chambers was sentenced to confinement for 3 years and 6 months, a dishonorable discharge, and reduction in rank to E-1.

Royal Air Force Lakenheath

United States v SSgt Patrick Huey

Base: RAF Lakenheath, UK

Synopsis: SSgt Huey was accused of sexually assaulting his local national girlfriend on multiple occasions between April 2006 and February 2008. The Air Force prosecuted this case after the local authorities decided not to proceed and relinquished jurisdiction to the Air Force.

Trial Results: On 29 Mar 12, at RAF Lakenheath, SSgt Huey was convicted by general court-martial of wrongful sexual contact and non-sexual assault offenses.

Adjudged Sentence: SSgt Huey was sentenced to confinement for 4 years and 9 months, a dishonorable discharge, and a reduction in rank to E-1.

United States v A1C Matthew B. Albright

Base: RAF Lakenheath AB, UK

Synopsis: In A1C Albright followed an intoxicated female airman back to her room and sexually assaulted her. On other occasions, A1C Albright entered another female airman's room while she slept and groped her in her sleep. A1C Albright was also found to be in possession of child pornography on his personal computer. Upon further investigation, investigators located one of the underage girls in the photos and learned that A1C Albright would masturbate while she exposed herself over the internet.

Trial Results: On 23 Mar 11, at Lakenheath AB, England, A1C Albright was convicted by general court-martial of wrongful sexual contact, indecent acts, 2 counts of unlawful entry, false official statement, willful dereliction of duty, and 2 counts of possession of child pornography.

Adjudged Sentence: A1C Albright was sentenced to confinement for 4 years, a dishonorable discharge, reduction in rank to E-1, and total forfeiture of all pay and allowances.

Note: The appropriate disposition to sexual assault allegations and investigations may not always include referral to trial by court-martial. Rather, some cases may be more appropriately handled through adverse administrative accountability actions. Additionally, adjudged sentences reported herein do not reflect any relief on the sentence that may have been granted upon appeal.

Little Rock Air Force Base

United States v SSgt Luis Tovar II

Base: Little Rock AFB, AR

Synopsis: In October 2011, SSgt Tovar sexually assaulted the female spouse of a military member who was substantially intoxicated and asleep.

Trial Results: On 4 May 12, at Little Rock AFB, AK, SSgt Tovar was convicted by general court-martial of wrongful sexual contact.

Adjudged Sentence: SSgt Tovar was sentenced to confinement 90 days, reduction in rank to E-2 and a reprimand.

Note: The appropriate disposition to sexual assault allegations and investigations may not always include referral to trial by court-martial. Rather, some cases may be more appropriately handled through adverse administrative accountability actions. Additionally, adjudged sentences reported herein do not reflect any relief on the sentence that may have been granted upon appeal.

Luke Air Force Base

United States v A1C Joe A. Montoya

Base: Luke AFB, AZ

Synopsis: A1C Montoya sexually assaulted an 18 year old female in his dorm room.

Trial Results: On 29 February 12, at Luke AFB, AZ, A1C Montoya was convicted by general court-martial of forcible sodomy and rape.

Adjudged Sentence: A1C Montoya was sentenced to confinement for 3 years and 6 months, a dishonorable discharge, reduction in rank to E-1, and total forfeiture of all pay and allowances.

Note: The appropriate disposition to sexual assault allegations and investigations may not always include referral to trial by court-martial. Rather, some cases may be more appropriately handled through adverse administrative accountability actions. Additionally, adjudged sentences reported herein do not reflect any relief on the sentence that may have been granted upon appeal.

Malmstrom Air Force Base

United States v AB Lee W. Payton, Jr.

Base: Malmstrom AFB, MT

Synopsis: After a night of drinking at local bars with friends, AB Payton drove a female Airman in the group home who was too drunk to drive. Once back at her dorm room, the female Airman invited AB Payton to spend the night in her suitemate's room. While she was asleep, AB Payton came into the female Airman's room and had sexual intercourse with her.

Trial Results: On 13 Jan 10, AB Payton was convicted by general court-martial of 2 counts of aggravated sexual assault.

Adjudged Sentence: AB Payton was sentenced to confinement for 5 years and 6 months, and a dishonorable discharge.

Note: The appropriate disposition to sexual assault allegations and investigations may not always include referral to trial by court-martial. Rather, some cases may be more appropriately handled through adverse administrative accountability actions. Additionally, adjudged sentences reported herein do not reflect any relief on the sentence that may have been granted upon appeal.

Maxwell Air Force Base

United States v Capt Matthew W. Swinney

Base: Maxwell AFB, AL

Synopsis: During a contentious divorce, evidence came to light that Capt Swinney sexually assaulted his wife and girlfriend.

Trial Results: On 12 Jan 11, Capt Swinney was convicted by general court-martial of abusive sexual contact, assault consummated by battery, indecent acts, communicating a threat, adultery, and disobeying an order.

Adjudged Sentence: Capt Swinney was sentenced to confinement for 7 months, dismissal, and total forfeitures of all pay and allowances.

Note: The appropriate disposition to sexual assault allegations and investigations may not always include referral to trial by court-martial. Rather, some cases may be more appropriately handled through adverse administrative accountability actions. Additionally, adjudged sentences reported herein do not reflect any relief on the sentence that may have been granted upon appeal.

Joint Base Lewis-McChord

United States v A1C James M. Boore

Base: JB Lewis-McChord, WA

Synopsis: A1C Boore sexually assaulted an intoxicated woman attending a party at his house.

Trial Results: On 9 Sep 11, A1C Boore was convicted by general court-martial of aggravated sexual assault on a person substantially incapacitated to appraise the nature of the sexual act, and willful dereliction of duty.

Adjudged Sentence: A1C Boore was sentenced to confinement for 6 months, a bad conduct discharge, and reduction in rank to E-1.

United States v SSgt Charles L. Walton

Base: JB Lewis-McChord, WA

Synopsis: SSgt Walton drove his new subordinate, a first-term female Airman, to the BX and then to her dorm room. The Airman invited SSgt Walton into her room to show her how to iron her uniform. While inside, SSgt Walton made sexual advances toward her and sexually assaulted her despite her protests.

Trial Results: On 25 Feb 10, SSgt Walton was convicted by general court-martial of forcible sodomy, assault, cruelty and maltreatment of a subordinate, and adultery.

Adjudged Sentence: SSgt Walton was sentenced to confinement for 1 year, a bad conduct discharge, and reduction in rank to E-2.

Note: The appropriate disposition to sexual assault allegations and investigations may not always include referral to trial by court-martial. Rather, some cases may be more appropriately handled through adverse administrative accountability actions. Additionally, adjudged sentences reported herein do not reflect any relief on the sentence that may have been granted upon appeal.

Joint Base McGuire-Dix-Lakehurst

United States v SSgt Jesse J. Harston

Base: JB McGuire-Dix-Lakehurst, NJ

Synopsis: SSgt Harston sexually assaulted a woman during a party where alcohol was involved.

Trial Results: On 14 Mar 12, SSgt Harston was convicted by general court-martial of aggravated sexual assault, forcible sodomy, and wrongful sexual contact.

Adjudged Sentence: SSgt Harston was sentenced to confinement for 6 years and reduction in rank to E-1.

Note: The appropriate disposition to sexual assault allegations and investigations may not always include referral to trial by court-martial. Rather, some cases may be more appropriately handled through adverse administrative accountability actions. Additionally, adjudged sentences reported herein do not reflect any relief on the sentence that may have been granted upon appeal.

Minot Air Force Base

United States v SSgt Edward M. Matteson

Base: Minot AFB, ND

Synopsis: During consensual horseplay between SSgt Matteson and his female subordinate at her house, SSgt Matteson sexually assaulted her.

Trial Results: On 14 Oct 10, at Minot AFB, ND, SSgt Matteson was convicted by special court-martial of aggravated sexual assault and assault consummated by a battery.

Adjudged Sentence: SSgt Matteson was sentenced to confinement for 20 days, reduction in rank to E-3, and a reprimand.

Note: The appropriate disposition to sexual assault allegations and investigations may not always include referral to trial by court-martial. Rather, some cases may be more appropriately handled through adverse administrative accountability actions. Additionally, adjudged sentences reported herein do not reflect any relief on the sentence that may have been granted upon appeal.

Moody Air Force Base

United States v TSgt Richard F. Greenwood

Base: Moody AFB, GA

Synopsis: TSgt Greenwood exposed himself to a female Air Force recruit and made unwanted sexual advances and exposed himself to other women.

Trial Results: On 16 Mar 12, TSgt Greenwood was convicted by general court-martial of indecent exposure, wrongful sexual contact, and dereliction of duty.

Adjudged Sentence: TSgt Greenwood was sentenced to confinement for 1 year, a dishonorable discharge, reduction in rank to E-1, and total forfeiture of all pay and allowances.

United States v A1C Bobby R. Rodriguez

Base: Moody AFB, GA

Synopsis: A1C Rodriguez sexually assaulted his friend's wife in their hotel room while she was incapacitated from alcohol consumption.

Trial Results: On 11 Feb 11, at Moody AFB, GA, A1C Rodriguez was convicted by general court-martial of aggravated sexual assault, and assault consummated by battery.

Adjudged Sentence: A1C Rodriguez was sentenced to confinement for 4 years, a dishonorable discharge, and reduction in rank to E-1.

United States v SSgt Deondre M. Ware

Base: Moody AFB, GA

Synopsis: As her new supervisor, SSgt Ware escorted a female Airman to their duty location, and then to her billeting room; all the while making sexually aggressive comments to the Airman. After helping her move into her billeting room, SSgt Ware sexually assaulted the Airman.

Note: The appropriate disposition to sexual assault allegations and investigations may not always include referral to trial by court-martial. Rather, some cases may be more appropriately handled through adverse administrative accountability actions. Additionally, adjudged sentences reported herein do not reflect any relief on the sentence that may have been granted upon appeal.

Trial Results: On 24 Mar 10, at Moody AFB, GA, SSgt Ware was convicted by special court-martial of wrongful sexual contact, cruelty and maltreatment of a subordinate, and making a false official statement.

Adjudged Sentence: SSgt Ware was sentenced to confinement for 9 months, a bad conduct discharge, reduction in rank to E-1, and forfeiture of $964.00 for 12 months.

Osan Air Base

United States v SrA Bradley J. Owens

Base: Osan AB, Republic of Korea

Synopsis: SrA Owens sexually assaulted a female airman when he forced sexual intercourse during otherwise consensual sexual activity.

Trial Results: On 12 Nov 11, at Osan AB, ROK, SrA Owens was convicted by general court-martial of aggravated sexual assault.

Adjudged Sentence: SrA Owens was sentenced to confinement for 1 year, a dishonorable discharge, and reduction in rank to E-1.

Note: The appropriate disposition to sexual assault allegations and investigations may not always include referral to trial by court-martial. Rather, some cases may be more appropriately handled through adverse administrative accountability actions. Additionally, adjudged sentences reported herein do not reflect any relief on the sentence that may have been granted upon appeal.

Peterson Air Force Base

United States v A1C Dustin A. Drees

Base: Peterson AFB, CO

Synopsis: A1C Drees had forcible sexual intercourse with a female airman, and performed oral sex on the wife of a deployed airman while she was passed out after drinking. On several other occasions, A1C Drees also engaged in several sex acts with 3 underage girls while at home in Iowa, and asked one of the girls not to tell investigators if they contacted her.

Trial Results: On 11 Mar 11, at Peterson AFB, CO, A1C Drees was convicted by general court-martial of aggravated sexual assault, indecent acts, sodomy, 3 counts of carnal knowledge of a child 12-16 years old, sodomy of a child 12-16 years old, 2 counts of obstructing justice, 2 counts of failure to obey a lawful order, and AWOL.

Adjudged Sentence: A1C Drees was sentenced to confinement for 8 years, a dishonorable discharge, reduction in rank to E-1, and total forfeiture of all pay and allowances.

Note: The appropriate disposition to sexual assault allegations and investigations may not always include referral to trial by court-martial. Rather, some cases may be more appropriately handled through adverse administrative accountability actions. Additionally, adjudged sentences reported herein do not reflect any relief on the sentence that may have been granted upon appeal.

Ramstein Air Base

United States v A1C Kevin N. Jones

Base: Ramstein AB, Germany

Synopsis: A1C Jones sexually assaulted a female friend at his home while they were drinking.

Trial Results: On 16 Sep 10, at Ramstein AB, Germany, A1C Jones was convicted by special court-martial of wrongful sexual contact.

Adjudged Sentence: A1C Jones was sentenced to confinement for 3 months, and reduction in rank to E-1.

Note: The appropriate disposition to sexual assault allegations and investigations may not always include referral to trial by court-martial. Rather, some cases may be more appropriately handled through adverse administrative accountability actions. Additionally, adjudged sentences reported herein do not reflect any relief on the sentence that may have been granted upon appeal.

Scott Air Force Base

United States v SSgt Reginald H. Norwood

Base: Scott AFB, IL

Synopsis: SSgt Norwood exposed himself to the victim while texting her at work.

Trial Results: On 23 January 12, at Scott AFB, IL, SSgt Norwood was convicted by special court-martial of indecent exposure.

Adjudged Sentence: SSgt Norwood was sentenced to confinement for 2 months, a bad conduct discharge, and reduction in rank to E-1.

Note: The appropriate disposition to sexual assault allegations and investigations may not always include referral to trial by court-martial. Rather, some cases may be more appropriately handled through adverse administrative accountability actions. Additionally, adjudged sentences reported herein do not reflect any relief on the sentence that may have been granted upon appeal.

Sheppard Air Force Base

United States v A1C Kenneth D. Beaver, II

Base: Sheppard AFB, TX

Synopsis: A1C Beaver sexually assaulted his roommate, a male Airman, while he slept.

Trial Results: On 17 Feb 10, at Sheppard AFB, TX, SrA Beaver was convicted by general court-martial of abusive sexual contact.

Adjudged Sentence: A1C Beaver was sentenced to confinement for 3 months, a bad conduct discharge, reduction in rank to E-1, and total forfeiture of all pay and allowances.

Note: The appropriate disposition to sexual assault allegations and investigations may not always include referral to trial by court-martial. Rather, some cases may be more appropriately handled through adverse administrative accountability actions. Additionally, adjudged sentences reported herein do not reflect any relief on the sentence that may have been granted upon appeal.

Tyndall Air Force Base

United States v SSgt James D. Friis

Base: Tyndall AFB, FL

Synopsis: SSgt Friis sexually assaulted his wife's visiting friend while she was sleeping in SSgt Friis's home.

Trial Results: On 22 Sep 10, at Tyndall AFB, FL, SSgt Friis was convicted by general court-martial of wrongful sexual contact.

Adjudged Sentence: SSgt Friis was sentenced to confinement for 6 months, a bad conduct discharge, and reduction in rank to E-1.

Note: The appropriate disposition to sexual assault allegations and investigations may not always include referral to trial by court-martial. Rather, some cases may be more appropriately handled through adverse administrative accountability actions. Additionally, adjudged sentences reported herein do not reflect any relief on the sentence that may have been granted upon appeal.

United States Air Force Academy

United States v. Cadet Stephan H. Claxton

Base: US Air Force Academy, CO

Synopsis: In Nov 11, Cadet Second Class (C2C) Claxton, attempted to sexually assault a female in his dorm room after they and a group of friends were drinking alcohol. When two other cadets prevented the assault, C2C Claxton physically assaulted the two cadets. During the investigation, it was revealed that C2C Claxton had also sexually assaulted a female cadet after a night of drinking in Mar 11.

Trial Results: On 22 Jun 12, at the Air Force Academy, CO, C2C Claxton was convicted by general court-martial of wrongful sexual contact, attempted abusive sexual contact, four counts of assault, and dereliction of duty for underage drinking.

Adjudged Sentence: C2C Claxton was sentenced to confinement for 6 months, a dismissal, and total forfeitures of all pay and allowances.

Note: The appropriate disposition to sexual assault allegations and investigations may not always include referral to trial by court-martial. Rather, some cases may be more appropriately handled through adverse administrative accountability actions. Additionally, adjudged sentences reported herein do not reflect any relief on the sentence that may have been granted upon appeal.

Vandenberg Air Force Base

United States v SrA Jeffrey Buller

Base: Vandenberg AFB, CA

Synopsis: SrA Buller took hidden video of a 17 year old female and transferred naked pictures of two other women from their electronic devices to his computer without their permission.

Trial Results: On 3 Apr 12, at Vandenberg AFB, SrA Buller was convicted by general court-martial of four specifications of indecent acts and non-sexual assault offenses.

Adjudged Sentence: SrA Buller was sentenced to confinement for 14 months, a bad conduct discharge, and a reduction in rank to E-1.

Note: The appropriate disposition to sexual assault allegations and investigations may not always include referral to trial by court-martial. Rather, some cases may be more appropriately handled through adverse administrative accountability actions. Additionally, adjudged sentences reported herein do not reflect any relief on the sentence that may have been granted upon appeal.

Wright-Patterson Air Force Base

United States v AB Larry Palmer

Base: Wright-Patterson AFB, OH

Synopsis: AB Palmer had sexual intercourse with victim while she was passing in and out of consciousness after he provided her with a series of alcoholic drinks.

Trial Results: On 24 May 12, AB Palmer was convicted by general court-martial of aggravated sexual assault on a person substantially incapacitated to appraise the nature of the sexual act, possession of a controlled substance, and making a false official statement.

Adjudged Sentence: AB Palmer was sentenced to a dishonorable discharge and 4 years confinement.